LETTERS

TO MY CHILDREN

JONATHAN JANSEN

LETTERS

TO MY CHILDREN

TWEETS TO MAKE YOU THINK

MACMILLAN

ISBN 978-1-920434-34-2

First edition, first impression 2012

Published jointly by
Bookstorm (Pty) Limited and Pan Macmillan South Africa

Suite 10
Private Bag X12
Cresta 2118
Johannesburg
South Africa
www.bookstorm.co.za

Private Bag X19
Northlands 2116
Johannesburg
South Africa
www.panmacmillan.co.za

Distributed by Pan Macmillan
Via Booksite Afrika

Edited by Pat Botes
Proofread by Aïda Thorne
Cover design by mr design
Cover photo by Stephen Collett
Typeset by Lebone Publishing Services
Printed and bound by Ultra Litho (Pty) Limited

To the mother of my children,
Grace, the real pedagogue

Contents

Before you start

Social media jargon

The letters in this collection were originally sent via *Facebook* and *Twitter*, I realise that not all the readers of this book will be familiar with these social networks, so here is a quick list of common jargon to help you decipher this new way of communicating (if you are already familiar with these skip over this section):

@: In *Twitter* the @ sign is used to call out usernames in tweets, like this: Hello @Twitter! When a username is preceded by the @ sign, it becomes a link to a *Twitter* profile.

Avatar: The personal image uploaded to your *Twitter* profile (it could be a picture of you or of something else).

Blog: A web log (you can use the word as a noun or a verb) – an online diary or column written by an individual.

Chat: A *Facebook* feature that lets users talk with friends (other users they know) who are using *Facebook* at the same time as they are.

Comment: *Facebook* users can comment on things that their friends say.

Direct message: On *Twitter* a direct message is a private message between the sender and the recipient.

Facebook: A network to share information with family, friends and other people you know or who know you.

Fan: A person who has joined a *Facebook* page because they like what that page represents.

Favorite (verb): On *Twitter* you can mark a tweet as one of your favourites by clicking the yellow star next to the message.

Follow (verb): To follow someone on *Twitter* is to subscribe to their tweets or updates on the site.

Follower (noun): A follower is another *Twitter* user who has followed you.

Following: Your following number shows the number of other *Twitter* users you have chosen to follow.

Friend: A person who has connected with a *Facebook* user, usually by invitation. Generally you have to be *Facebook* friends before someone can see what you have written.

Handle: A user's *Twitter* handle is the username he or she has selected.

Hashtag: In *Twitter* the # symbol, called a hashtag, is used to mark keywords or topics in a tweet. It was created by *Twitter* users as a way to categorise messages.

Like: The Like button occurs next to content on *Facebook* and

allows users to let others know they appreciate that content (a video, a comment, a photo or something else).

Mention (noun): When you mention (verb) another *Twitter* user in your tweet by including the @ sign followed directly by their username. It also refers to tweets in which your username was included.

Poke (noun or verb): You can give a friend on *Facebook* a virtual 'poke' to say hello, congratulate them, etc.

Profile: A *Facebook* profile is a *Facebook* site created by people who want to share information about themselves and socialise with others. A *Facebook* profile shows a user's personal information and their interactions with friends. A *Twitter* profile is a *Twitter* page displaying information about a user, as well as all the tweets they have posted from their account.

Reply: On *Twitter* a tweet posted in reply to another user's message.

Retweet (noun): A tweet by another *Twitter* user, forwarded to you by someone you follow. Often used to spread news or share valuable findings on *Twitter*.

Retweet (verb): To retweet, retweeting, retweeted. The act of forwarding another *Twitter* user's tweet to all of your followers. Abbreviated to RT.

Share: *Facebook* users can share content from their friends' pages with other friends.

Status: Your *Facebook* status is a feature which allows you as user to inform your friends of your current whereabouts, actions or thoughts.

Status update: Changing your status on *Facebook* sends a message to your friends about your new thoughts, etc.

Tag: On *Facebook* you can mark a photo or video with text that identifies the person featured in the photo or video.

Trending topic: A subject algorithmically determined to be one of the most popular on *Twitter* at the moment.

Tweet (noun): A message posted via *Twitter* containing 140 characters or fewer.

Tweet (verb): Tweet, tweeting, tweeted. The act of posting a message, often called a tweet, on *Twitter*.

Tweeter: A *Twitter* account holder who posts and reads tweets. Also known as twitterers.

Twitter: An information network made up of 140-character messages from all over the world.

Twitter name: The name a user calls him or herself on *Twitter*.

Twitterer: A *Twitter* account holder who posts and reads tweets. Also known as a *Twitter* user.

Unfollow: To stop following another *Twitter* user.

Unfriend: To remove a *Facebook* user from your list of *Facebook* friends so they can no longer see your content.

Wall: Every *Facebook* profile has a wall which allows friends and users themselves to post messages for all to see.

Introduction

Blame my favourite writer. You have not 'felt' writing unless you've read Maya Angelou, the great African-American author, poet and activist who wrote a famous book called *I know why the caged bird sings*. But it was her *Letter to my daughter* that really got my attention. As I read her letter I could not think of a greater gift to offer my own children than the life lessons I've learnt from hard experience. Now of course our parents (and other elders) leave all of us letters, so to speak, by which I mean those sayings we call to mind in later years in the form of 'my mother always used to say that ...' or 'my father's favourite line was ...', and so on.

With this in mind, I decided to put onto paper my own letters to my two inspiring children, Mikhail and Sara-Jane, over a period of 365 days, i.e. a letter for every day of the calendar year. But of course this was not only for my two biological children; it was a way of communicating some core commitments to my more than 30 000 other 'children' at the University of the Free State, and the many who followed what I was trying to convey about schools and the country through public forums such as the Thursday column in *The Times*.

The letters were issued daily through two social media, Twitter and Facebook, and what I did not expect was the intense response they elicited. My Facebook page quickly reached the 5 000 'friends' limit and Twitter followers swelled to more than 11 000 after my first 100 tweets. There were a few reasons for the choice of social media to communicate these messages. It was a way of conveying a sense of being in touch with my students, many of whom I would never meet physically given the three University of the Free State campuses, at varying distances from my office. It was, to my students at least, a sure sign of being 'cool' (I heard that many times) for logging onto the latest technologies with which young people are so adept. It is also the most efficient mechanism for mass communication in real time; sitting at the airport waiting for a delayed flight, I enjoyed the fact that I could use my cellphone to answer 60 questions with single-line responses and post the Twitter messages for the next day. Now isn't that cool? I confess I find the stops at red robots or a slow drive in

heavy traffic a wonderful opportunity to respond to a few quick Twitter or Facebook inquiries without having to lug a laptop around with me. I can hear you saying: 'He's no example to the youth.' True.

Social media make me realise how ridiculous it is in the twenty-first century to have students and parents queuing (and recently even dying) in lines to register for university admissions. Our universities are like massive old ships that struggle to turn in heavy waters in response to computer-generated images that replaced the old lighthouse on the shore. What the social media do for me is to close the physical distance between leaders and followers, or between managers and clients; they convey a sense of emotional connection to those you serve. I would love to see which South African university will be the first to have a paperless and queueless registration process using the power of new media for this purpose.

The daily letter took the form of a short statement of a precious lesson I learnt somewhere on the road of life. The scope of lessons covered subjects ranging from leadership to learning, about love and living, concerning schools and the workplace, on public service and materialism, and from 'how to drive' to 'how to leave the country' while your body remains at home. *'Jy het 'n moeilike perd opgesaal'*

(literally, 'you have mounted a difficult horse') said one of the campus dominees, correctly predicting the difficulty of committing to a new letter every single day.

There were such days. I would rise in the early morning and think, 'Oh no, what letter should I issue today?' My task was not made easier when an unknown mother put pressure on me in cyberspace with this veiled 'hurry-up' announcement: 'I wait for your letter every morning so that I can read it to my children before they leave for school.' I suspect that the pressure to produce these letters, and in two media, is one of the reasons why the numbering of the letters sometimes fell out of sequence; I apologise for that, and hope this book helps to overcome the problem.

I discovered something very interesting in this process. The more I reached for other people's lessons, the more I came up empty. The more I relied on my own experiences, the more authentic the letters. I recalled things my father or mother taught me. I remembered the hardships I experienced growing up. I dug up hurtful memories from childhood. I revelled in those many moments of overcoming difficult situations. I reminded myself of the mistakes I had made and which I could have avoided. And the more I went back into the memory bank, the easier the flow of thought became that resulted in letters.

'Nothing completely new here,' mused one cyberfriend, 'just that he puts it differently.' I suspect it's true that, over the centuries, wiser people must have thought of these lessons before. I could only hope that the letters came across as fresh and inspiring to the people who read them. The comments certainly indicate that this might be so. 'This was just what I needed for the day,' someone would often respond after an early morning release of a letter. The fact that the letters encouraged ordinary people whom I had never met was the single most important reason I kept posting them.

But I realised that, if I were true to myself, the letters would invariably split the followers. In this respect, after some time I found it possible to anticipate which letter would bring 'like' responses on Facebook and which would bring 'comment' responses. A simple, straightforward, uncontroversial tweet or posting would bring 100 or more 'likes' on Facebook or simple 'RTs' (retweets) on Twitter. But it was also clear to me that these were the least helpful kinds of postings. After all, a large part of my teaching identity is tied to the notion of not confirming people's knowledge or beliefs but challenging, even disrupting, them. It was even more fun watching the anxiety over meaning; after all, the idea was not to spell out exactly what I meant with a particular posting, but in fact to leave some room for interpretation. This was not good enough for many followers: 'Say what you mean' or 'Please clarify' or 'I'm confused' were not uncommon responses. But that would defeat the whole purpose.

It was frustrating, though, to see some influential figures deliberately distort a simple message, like the letter I posted on the weekend of the ANC's hundredth birthday celebrations in Mangaung, Bloemfontein, which read: 'Always remember that no one political party or movement or ethnic group brought your country its freedom.' One prominent activist responded swiftly: 'Jansen is wrong because our freedom would not have been won without the ANC,' and when some of his followers pointed out the obvious, that both our statements could be true, he reacted with another absurdity, 'Jansen's statement is an attempt to create equivalence.'

Once this African nationalist fervour has died down after the ANC centenary, I really hope that our history books record the many movements, organisations and individuals over the centuries that chipped away at the certainties of colonialism and the rigidities of apartheid, not only in South Africa but also in the region, on the continent, and across the world. That the ANC in the twentieth century stands tall among the other struggle movements is undeniable, but I have yet to encounter a deeply thoughtful, nuanced and honest account of the history of this impressive organisation that was started by well-dressed, well-educated, decent gentlemen in the early twentieth century. I also hope that such an historical account, stripped of hyperbole, will explain how this noble movement, which has done so much for our country, degenerated into the kind of tortured, hypersensitive, angry, grasping lot we have today.

Yet no single posting generated more turmoil than the deliberately ambiguous letter consisting of two words: 'Condoms break.'

'Does the professor condone promiscuity? Of course condoms break, but usually not if you use them correctly. Students *should* use condoms; it is the only effective way to combat the spread of that virus. Young people will have sex anyway, so give them condoms'. I enjoyed the range of responses as people struggled with extracting meaning from the two-word dilemma.

Sooner or later the two-word conundrum would become the butt of national jokes. The Minister of Sport (truly) was found to have impregnated a stranger in the period he was temporarily estranged from his wife. He blamed an 'exploding condom' and there was even the suggestion that the rubber was tampered with in a honey trap set by the National Intelligence Agency to prevent him from becoming ANC Secretary-General at the 2012 elective conference of a party whose leaders scored more hits in unfamiliar bedrooms than in municipal service delivery. 'Condoms break!' several of my naughty followers reminded the Minister of Sport (and Recreation?).

This is a big thing on university campuses, this condom thing. In conversation with a senior colleague at a Durban university, the official informed me that at their institution 60 000 condoms are taken for use every month. 'No wonder there is so much friction on your campus,' I suggested, since this university was in constant turmoil over everything from student accommodation to tuition fees to, yes, a protest to replace government-issued condoms with brand-name condoms. I kid you not.

If sex did not stir the followers, politics succeeded. This is where the abuse set in. One tweet instructs my children never to take a job if they suspect that the offer was based on skin colour advantage. The name-calling started. I was denying apartheid. Whites had got it that way; why not blacks. This shows that Jansen is really a neoliberal, a conservative, a coconut … I lost track of the insults. Sticks and stones. I was expected to follow the angry black line in public commentary, not think for myself.

As black folk we do not even realise how we demean ourselves by playing into this game of needing a hand to make it in a country whose government is run by people who look like us. We fail to see how we are using the very tactics of the despicable apartheid state to achieve and acquire, once again, on the basis of the epidermis.

My problem is that I have seen far too many talented black South Africans in this country and across the world who are as good as and better than their white compatriots in any job to believe we need to humiliate ourselves by pandering to skin colour. My academic and occupational standard-bearers are Biko and Sobukwe, not Malema and Zuma. I revel in the examples of Richard Rive, Charlotte Maxeke and Fatima Meer, not in the slothful examples of bitter people whose only means for getting ahead is to do what the whites once did and enforce affirmative action over natural intelligence and God-given talents. Talent is normally distributed, I would often remind my more angry students for whom 'learnt helplessness' has already become a regular part of their political diet.

At the heart of this new black politics in South Africa is the insistence, by both white and black people, that there is one kind of black man or woman who understands the pulse of the masses: the inarticulate person with a distinctly

'African' accent and limited education. This particularly nasty nativism finds common purpose across the political spectrum. My more conservative white compatriots find relief in reinforcing the racial stereotype that all blacks are the same, this of course justifies the 'Western' (I still hear some whites refer to themselves as such) and more sophisticated Other, themselves. I used to stare in shock at Afrikaans bigots who would poke fun openly at black English speakers at language-promotion conferences with the obvious inference that 'dark skins should speak black languages'. The dogged pursuit of ethno-genetic differences satisfies some deep, resilient racism in all of us: *hulle is (nog steeds) nie soos ons nie* (they are still not like us).

On the other hand, my more liberal white counterparts play exactly the same game. Who can forget Stephen Friedman's sickening attack on Lindiwe Mazibuko, newly elected leader of the parliamentary opposition, whom he described as someone chosen because she spoke with a white accent and was therefore acceptable in class and culture to the Democratic Party. There is just no way, in Friedman's warped thinking, that Mazibuko could simply be the most competent candidate, 'finish and klaar'. No, excellence and attainment on the part of black people must be qualified as a particular kind of excellence that is epidermal, first and last.

If he had pondered this thoughtless statement, Friedman would have realised he was in exactly the same camp of tribalist thinking as Malema, who poked fun at a member of his own party – Minister Naledi Pandor – for not speaking like an authentic black as she has an English-trained accent. She was not, like Mazibuko, a real black.

One understands of course how pseudo-radicals within black majority politics would seek to attack and demean any black who dares to think outside of the racial box. They are the kind of people who beat up other blacks who have a different view on a strike action. Blacks are beaten into submission by other blacks. Anyone black who does not belong to the dominant party is abnormal and therefore a perfect candidate for slander and attack.

Where does this behaviour come from? The apartheid system of course. One of my enduring memories was how the apartheid courts dealt with especially white women activists who were found guilty of supporting the liberation movements. The only defence that seemed to get through the racial hard-heads on the bench was that the accused was either overweight with low self-esteem or ignorant to the point of having been brainwashed. The obvious answer that the person was intelligent enough to make up her own mind and act on a healthy conscience was just too much for the white nationalists to bear. Get it? The black nationalists today reason in precisely the same way.

What the letters do, of course, is to challenge this kind of essentialist thinking, but there was the dilemma of personal exposure. The letters reveal the author's politics. A single letter resulted in followers declaring their 'aha's' as if there was some great revelation of a black conservative or a comrade after all. Opinions went back and forth, and I hope that what readers conclude from these letters is a set of public commitments that do not submit readily to our South African obsession with categorisation. I would love my epitaph to read, 'Unclassifiable.'

The most difficult letters to write concerned the English. This is a taboo topic in polite South Africa. After all, the English were all liberals who opposed apartheid, right? They are, after all, not like our stereotyped Afrikaner who is an undeniable rustic racist with shorts and brown-striped clothing, right? What a load of nonsense! And yet when Jacob Zuma made some mildly critical reference to the English, all hell broke loose. Letter #16 was therefore difficult to compose, but the point stands: 'You will hear in black circles that you can trust the Afrikaner more than the English; trust them both.'

That said, we need to talk about the English and 'the illusion of innocence' about their role in the past.

Many of the old liberals were vociferous in their stance against all black people voting; we tend to forget that. The institutionalised racism of universities like Cape Town and Wits played their part in limiting black student enrolments and in hiring top black scholars even when there was no duress from the apartheid state. Black students to this day will tell you of exclusion and alienation within these pretentious, anglicised cultures of learning. But we dare not ruffle the English feathers; it is so much easier to pull up our noses at the Afrikaans universities. In his book, *The English: A portrait of a people*, Jeremy Paxman asks a simple question: 'Where did they get their extraordinary capacity for hypocrisy?' It is a question worth pursuing in the new South Africa, about others, and oneself.

This brings me to the question of the personal meanings of the advice contained in so many letters. I regularly asked my two biological children for their honest opinion on one or other letter. The 'honest' bit is unnecessary, of course, since, like all children, they are ruthless in their feedback to their parents. It was after one such query that my son responded firmly and with a slight smile across his face: 'This [the advice in a letter] coming from a man who …'. I do not remember the specific letter, but it was an opportunity then, and now, to set the record straight.

But first, what I love about teenagers is their suspicion of their parents. They watch you like a hawk, and they know more about you than they care to reveal. I learnt early on not to preach to my children about right or wrong but rather to try to demonstrate, imperfectly, what the better life could look like – in terms of common decencies, race relations, attitudes towards women, respect for elders, and a healthy dose of scepticism about authority. My own children have been privileged to have the best of mothers who mixes love and discipline in a perfect cocktail of childrearing common sense, and her work compensated for my weaknesses as a father. For this reason, the book belongs to their real teacher, their mother.

And so my response to my children is that I have fallen foul of many of the concerns or pieces of advice offered in these letters. The letters come from a fallen man, an imperfect father, a broken leader. It is precisely what I have learnt from doing wrong, and sometimes right; that became the motivation for the letters.

I once hated white people, and I am ashamed about that. I once cheated in a high school test, and I wish I could retrace those steps when I wrote the sine and cosine equations on the back of the legitimate logbook one could use in the exam room. I once slept in a hotel as a young man and the cheque bounced; when I went back to pay in cash years later they refused to take the money, saying they no longer had a record of the rubber cheque. I could continue with a long list of things I am ashamed of. And so I write not out of a sense of moral superiority, but with a burden to warn about the potholes on the road of life, especially the ones that shatter the tyre threads of your conscience.

There are important lessons about the importance of making mistakes. As one letter puts it, 'Go to university to screw-up; how else will you learn?' I believe that our paucity of leadership in science, engineering and innovation has its roots in our collective culture of fear – the fear of making mistakes, of standing out, of being contrary. We teach our children to colour in inside the Foundation Phase circles and reprimand them for solving a mathematical problem in fewer than the teacher-required steps. This conformity is deeply embedded in school and society, and hence the aversion to risk among children and adults alike. The messages in these letters convey the opposite.

The responses to my tweets that I had most difficulty with were the ones in which rage replaced reason. I am a university professor. I am paid to think. I do not have a lot of money nor do I pay attention to things like social status.

My parents died poor and left us very little in terms of material possessions. The only thing I have is reason. And so, I confess, I do not do well with unreason.

Imagine my shock when I read the responses to Letter #39: 'It is not true that all whites supported apartheid; nor is it true that all blacks were against it.' Several black followers hyperventilated when they read this tweet, if the acidic comments are anything to go by. Yet it is so true, and recognising this simple fact has major implications for how we think about the past, navigate the present, and imagine the future.

It is not only the well-known, heroic white compatriots – Slovo, Kasrils, Sachs, Fischer, First, Aggett – who shared and suffered in the struggle against colonialism and apartheid. We have yet to see books about the ordinary, below-the-radar white citizens who formed part of the moral underground, housing activists, feeding families of inmates, helping young people over the border, and depositing funds into faraway accounts to help those in the liberation movements. I know many of them who will never get a single word of recognition for their vital part in past struggles. That the overwhelming numbers of whites benefited from and voted for white rule is not in question; that is a fact. But that thousands in visible and invisible ways stood in solidarity against racial rule is also something we need to acknowledge.

And then, of course, the sore point: the many black people who thrived on apartheid. One of the great tragedies of thin reconciliation is how we covered up the sell-outs who participated in the Tricameral Parliament, the black councillors who gave slim credibility to fake urban councils, and the homeland leaders who made their wealth on the back of these rural slums. What about all those black policemen who laboured alongside their white superiors to mow down black citizens? Where did all these people go, and why are we so reluctant to talk about black participation in white rule?

What the letters on this subject tried to do, of course, was to introduce complexity into the established narrative of the past. The white evil – black good trope has run its short course. There are far too many shades of grey in that moral struggle against racism and racial rule that need to be studied and shared, for I witness too often the anger of latter-day youth who did not experience a single day of apartheid but fight their anti-white struggles with this simple view of history in their heads.

Where the letters, as well as general comments on Facebook in particular, drew a discernible anger was when they talked about everyday racism. Legalised racism is gone; there is a Constitution and a Bill of Rights that defend us, and a somewhat hobbling Human Rights Commission to run to. The big violations make the news. The everyday racism of South Africa does not.

The summer of 2011/12 will remain one of the most disturbing in my post-1994 memory. For some reason, I found myself in all kinds of dangerous situations that I certainly had not encountered in such a short space of time before. Let me take you through some of them, all in that incomparably beautiful city of my childhood, youth and early adulthood, Cape Town.

It was the Kenilworth pharmacist who treated the black couple two places ahead of me in the queue with cold efficiency, then apologised profusely to the white woman who followed for the fact that she had to stand in a long line, and when my turn came, it was back to the same icy attitude. The next day we took a drive to Kalk Bay for dinner and came around Boyes Drive for the return trip to the southern suburbs. The police officer shone a torch into my eyes, and kept it there, forcing me to stop to ask for directions, only to be met with the kind of verbal abuse I last suffered by apartheid's cops. What really got to me was that while he was screaming at me he would break from his tirade at regular intervals to warmly greet and guide the equally confused white motorists behind me, with torch pointing towards the ground. The following day I entered a major bookshop in Claremont only to be followed down every passage by the security guard who has to pretend he is not one; I stopped at the shelf holding my four recently published books and offered him a signed copy. He has done this to me often before but after the Kenilworth and Kalk Bay experiences, I became aware that he does not follow my pale-skinned brothers.

What makes these manifestations of everyday prejudice so interesting is that all three perpetrators – the pharmacist, the cop and the security hand – were black. What is equally fascinating is that I largely escape this kind of harassment when I dress as a middle-class man or am recognised as a university principal. In these cases, dressed in shorts with old shoes and a slightly grubby T-shirt, I was just another black man. And what also makes these confrontations – I raised my ire with all three men – so intriguing, is that they all happened in Cape Town at about the same time that its leading politician was in an intense set of exchanges on the social media on that perennial question from those quarters, 'Is Cape Town racist?'

There is a structure of prejudice in beautiful Cape Town that is a lot more complex (African, coloured, white; Afrikaans, English; Muslim, Christian, Jewish; very rich, very poor; the legacy of slavery alongside colonialism and apartheid; the sheer Englishness of the place, polite in its brutality) than in the other provinces. One consequence of this complex history is the ways in which black functionaries are victims of white power, subjects of white privilege, and conveyors of white prejudice. And then there is the issue of social class, something that matters enormously in the Cape as an unspoken legacy of English colonialism, where how you dress or speak or carry yourself, or simply appear, gets the kind of treatment described above.

This has been one of the most exciting ventures that I have embarked on in many years. I simply love the media and enjoyed the many and varied responses to the letters. I found that the most powerful facility on Facebook was 'unfriend' and any abusive or illogical responses were easily deleted. I will continue this engagement, and while this book reports the first batch of letters, readers are invited to keep following these crisp wisdoms through to the target of 365 letters.

I must thank you all for enriching my life and thinking through positive and critical responses.

To conclude, it should be clear from the Facebook and Twitter exchanges that we still need to talk, and what the letters do is to signal directions for talking ourselves out of the trouble that faces us if we do not. If the letters succeed in this purpose, this project will have been more than worthwhile.

Jonathan Jansen
February 2012

Letters to my
children

Letters to my children #1

Be cautious about people who call you comrade; they want something.

Letters to my children #2

Never sing the national anthem without thinking; you might just end up hating foreigners.

Letters to my children #3

Condoms break.

Letters to my children #4

Never under any circumstances become a politician; choose public service instead.

Letters to my children #5

Here is the secret to dealing with peer
pressure – choose the right peers.

Letters to my children #6

Go to university to screw-up; how else will you learn?

Letters to my children #7

Do not judge poor people with too many children; they might be the only gifts they have.

Letters to my children #8

Speak more than one language; it will improve your love life.

Letters to my children #9

Never let anyone force you to choose
between your white brother and your
black brother; choose your brother.

Letters to my children #10

My only instruction to you is this –
ignore those four racial boxes on forms
and write the word HUMAN.

Letters to my children #11

Avoid people who are too sure
of themselves; life is a lot more
interesting.

Letters to my children #12

Keep your hands off your children,
for parents who beat their children are
cowards.

Letters to my children #13

Sex is overrated; love is not.

Letters to my children #14

You are not coloured. We all are – it's what you'd expect after 350 years of sleeping together.

Letters to my children #15

No matter what they do to your body,

protect your soul at all times.

Letters to my children #16

You will hear in black circles that you can trust the Afrikaner more than the English; trust them both.

Letters to my children #17

It is your duty, as it is that of every generation, to do better than your parents.

Letters to my children #18

Trust your gut; most times it's right.

Letters to my children #19

I know of no greater joy than to give your money to those in greater need.

Letters to my children #20

In South Africa whistle-blowers lose their jobs; whistle anyway.

Letters to my children #21

Do not only tolerate those who are
different from you; embrace them.

Letters to my children #22

If you even suspect you are getting a
job because of your skin, say 'no thank
you'; we taught you self-respect.

Letters to my children #23

A loud, aggressive man is frightened of something; find out what, and you will have won.

Letters to my children #24

No matter who your audience, speak simply; people who use big words are insecure.

Letters to my children #25

I can now reveal to you what has kept
me going during the most difficult
times in my life: Deuteronomy 33 v 27.

Letters to my children #26

Do not judge people who commit
suicide; they might be the most honest
among us.

Letters to my children #27

If your partner ever lifts his/her
hand to hurt you, leave him/her
permanently – for it will happen again.

Letters to my children #28

Disadvantage is primarily in the mind;

tell yourself you are, and you will be.

Letters to my children #29

Be suspicious of crowds; learn to think for yourself.

Letters to my children #30

No matter how dark and difficult your circumstances, remember this: you are not alone.

Letters to my children #31

If someone tells you to get lost, do so; you'll be surprised what you find along the way.

Letters to my children #32

Never, ever, argue with a bigot; it is the
easiest way to demean yourself.

Letters to my children #33

Never lose that feeling of discomfort when you witness inequality.

Letters to my children #34

You will come this way only once;

make sure to leave your mark.

Letters to my children #35

Sex is for marriage.

Letters to my children #36

The key to successful leadership is discovering your own brokenness.

Letters to my children #37

I need you to know that the greatest joy
I have ever experienced was having the
two of you as my children.

Letters to my children #38

It does not matter how often you fall;
what matters most is that you stand up
every time.

Letters to my children #39

It is not true that all whites supported apartheid; nor is it true that all blacks were against it.

Letters to my children #40

You have absolutely no idea what capacity for greatness lies within you.

Letters to my children #41

When you take a stand on principle, people might not love you but they will respect you.

Letters to my children #42

If all your friends look like you, believe like you, love and live like you – your life will be impoverished.

Letters to my children #43

The most dangerous thing you can do is to make decisions when you're angry.

Letters to my children #44

Work hard, but take time often to restore your soul through music, laughter and friends.

Letters to my children #45

_____

Amidst all the busyness with the detail
of life, stop often to ask the big-picture
question – why am I here; why am I
doing this?

Letters to my children #46

You are not fully human until you can feel the pain of those whom you think are different from you.

Letters to my children #47

The best way to achieve a balanced, unselfish life is to have your own children.

Letters to my children #48

The kind of man your daughter marries
will depend on how you treat your wife.

Letters to my children #49

Never put your children on Ritalin®; it is too often a cultural suppressant for a joyful life.

Letters to my children #50

If your followers know you would die for them, the rest of your job as a leader is easy.

Letters to my children #51

Even atheists believe in something.

Letters to my children #52

South Africa does not need you; you need this country to teach you humility, compassion and public service.

Letters to my children #53

No matter how high you soar in life, I want you to keep your feet solidly on the ground.

Letters to my children #54

Try to keep your life simple; the more material things you acquire, the more headaches you get.

Letters to my children #55

I can tell you that I have gained more wisdom from people with no schooling than knowledge from people with degrees.

Letters to my children #56

Your humanity is enhanced every time you do that most difficult thing – which is to say 'I'm sorry, I did wrong'.

Letters to my children #57

We all are born with a gene for
revenge; locate it early in your personal
DNA.

Letters to my children #58

Curiosity did not kill the cat; it was
reckless.

Letters to my children #59

Learn the skills of 'crap detection' early; it will save you needless pain.

Letters to my children #60

Whenever some jerk tells you what you
cannot do, take that as a challenge.

Letters to my children #61

It really is not important what you
wear, what you drive, or what you own;
what matters is what you are.

Letters to my children #62

Whenever people praise you, redirect that praise to those who made you and your achievements possible.

Letters to my children #63

When faced with a difficult ethical
decision, err on the side of caution.

Letters to my children #64

Nobody ever won the Nobel Prize for following the established wisdom; think and live against the grain.

Letters to my children #65

My life changed when I realised I could excel on four hours' sleep per night; sleep is a learnt behaviour.

Letters to my children #66

Be absolutely honest with everyone
around you; but I warn you, timing is
everything.

Letters to my children #67

_____

Don't waste your time playing the

Lotto; create your own luck.

Letters to my children #68

Bad things happen; the sooner you accept that, the easier it will be to enjoy the good things that also happen.

Letters to my children #69

A leader needs both a soft hand and a hard hand; the secret is to know when to use which hand.

Letters to my children #70

There is no such thing as a perfect team; even Jesus had a dropout.

Letters to my children #71

The measure of your leadership lies in how you respond to a crisis.

Letters to my children #72

Once a week, look in a mirror, and ask this simple question: 'Am I absolutely honest with myself?'

Lessons to my children #73

The hardest lesson I had to learn was
to respect my parents at all times,
especially when they were wrong.

Letters to my children #74

Under no circumstances allow yourself
to be intimidated by anyone, no matter
how wealthy, how famous or how
angry.

Letters to my children #75

You are not a real man until you learn
to cry.

Letters to my children #76

Beware of people who use the word
transformation when what they really
mean is domination.

Letters to my children #77

Never lose your sense of awe of the simple things of beauty that surround you.

Letters to my children #78

Know the difference between life
and living, between house and home,
between spouse and lover.

Letters to my children #79

There is no such thing as a problem child; only problem parents.

Letters to my children #80

I discovered that it is possible to emigrate without your body leaving the country.

Letters to my children #81

Your loyalty must never be to a country
or a government, but to ideals worth
living for.

Letters to my children #82

You will survive on the roads if you
assume the other driver is an idiot.

Letters to my children #83

Do not test the hot-cold taps while standing under the shower.

Letters to my children #84

Treat your secretary with respect; she is the most powerful person in any organisation. She can make or break you.

Letters to my children #85

It is not true that the Earth is overpopulated; the problem is that resources are unequally distributed.

Letters to my children #86

Measure your overall health in terms of when you last had a hearty laugh from the pit of your stomach.

Letters to my children #87

If you keep the same job for more than seven years, you clearly have no imagination.

Letters to my children #88

There are some family members you will only meet at funerals; that is not necessarily a bad thing.

Letters to my children #89

Think of anti-racism the way you think about antibiotics; there will always be resistant bugs.

Letters to my children #90

You will save yourself a lot of confusion by simply accepting that there are more than two genders.

Letters to my children #91

Those politicians who insist on talking about the South African revolution have clearly not lived through one.

Letters to my children #92

When they tell you that you did not
get a job because you do not fit in, the
problem lies with them, not you.

Letters to my children #93

The most lasting damage of apartheid was to give all South Africans – black and white – a deep inferiority complex.

Letters to my children #94

Do not, in your anger, destroy former white universities; you will need them for your grandchildren.

Letters to my children #95

I love only two things in life – eating and writing. Nobody has ever asked me where I find the time to eat.

Letters to my children #96

Distinguish two things in life: the crisis, and how you respond to it. The crisis is not the problem.

Letters to my children #97

You will be surprised how many great men stumble because of that little appendage.

Letters to my children #98

The fact that you gave birth to children does not make you parents; a parent is much more than biology.

Letters to my children #99

You know you have landed the perfect job when you hate Fridays and love Mondays.

Letters to my children #100

Resist the pressure to say something profound simply because you have reached one or other milestone.

Letters to my children #101

Tell the waiter the food sucks; learn the habit of speaking your mind.

Letters to my children #102

If your partner says 'don't worry with a gift for me this year', and you don't, you will pay a heavy price.

Letters to my children #103

A person who starts a sentence with 'to be honest with you' is probably not.

Letters to my children #104

Of course you stand on the shoulders
of giants; but you'll get nowhere if you
don't also stamp on their toes.

Letters to my children #105

Be careful what you commit to
memory; it can come back to haunt you
in later life.

Letters to my children #106

Here is the best financial advice for a young person: buy a house before you buy a car.

Letters to my children #107

Do not chase your children out of adult
company; if you do, they'll struggle
with confidence among adults later.

Letters to my children #108

Every family has a scandal and a scoundrel it does not want to talk about.

Letters to my children #109

Do not go through life without a
designated mentor; it is too risky
without one.

Letters to my children #110

I have never smoked a cigarette; I have never drunk wine; but no, you are not adopted.

Letters to my children #111

You cannot demand that your children respect you.

Letters to my children #112

Learn to give when you have nothing to offer.

Letters to my children #113

The difference between having schooling and having education is the number of books you read.

Letters to my children #114

Now and again attend a place of worship completely outside of your own faith; it will make you more fully human.

Letters to my children #115

Let's get one thing straight:
grandparents are not dumping grounds
for children you did not plan to have.

Letters to my children #116

Never, ever, overtake behind a car that is overtaking.

Letters to my children #117

If you fall asleep while driving, there's a good chance you will not wake up again.

Letters to my children #118

There is no such thing as African time;

only wasting other people's time.

Letters to my children #119

You can put this in the bank – South Africans are among the laziest people in the world.

Letters to my children #120

People who give you criticism either
intend to help you or to hurt you; know
which one is which.

Letters to my children #121

There is no such thing as falling in
love; if you do, you'll knock your head.

Letters to my children #122

What you eat now will determine your quality of life when you're older; on the other hand, you could be hit by a bus.

Letters to my children #123

There's a reason they play Christmas
music in the malls – so that you can
relax the grip on your wallet.

Letters to my children #124

Do not judge too harshly someone who takes drugs; it might be the only escape from a miserable life.

Letters to my children #125

When you marry, ask for money; it will stop people recycling cheap gifts.

Letters to my children #126

There's a more than 50 per cent chance you will meet a sibling you did not know about at your father's funeral.

Letters to my children #127

There's a more than 90 per cent chance that you have black/white blood in your veins.

Letters to my children #128

When you learn to forgive you relieve
yourself of pain and add years to your
life.

Letters to my children #129

Here's perspective – you cannot build a better past; only a better future (thanks Claude).

Letters to my children #130

Take time to rest; your company will not show up at your funeral.

Letters to my children #131

No matter what you do, Christmas is just not the same without your mother.

Letters to my children #132

I learnt from my blind grandfather to distinguish sight from insight.

Letters to my children #133

There is nothing worse than pretense;

be yourself, always.

Letters to my children #134

The people who stick with you AFTER you've messed up are called friends.

Letters to my children #135

There is a peace that passes all understanding.

Letters to my children #136

When you feel the need to check your partner's cellphone on the sly, know that your relationship is in trouble.

Letters to my children #137

Despite the risk of history, always
present yourself as a servant.

Letters to my children #138

Do not tell people what you are
prepared to die for; tell them what you
are prepared to live for.

Letters to my children #139

Do not live your life apologetically; people will sense it and walk all over you.

Letters to my children #140

Do not waste your time making meaningless resolutions; just do the right thing.

Letters to my children #141

There is no such thing as destiny; you make your own with the grace you receive.

Letters to my children #142

Unlearn the South African habit of confusing discipline with punishment.

Letters to my children #143

There is nothing more enlightened than cross-cultural adoptions.

Letters to my children #144

The human mind has the incredible

capacity for self-deception.

Letters to my children #145

Always remember that no single party
or movement or ethnic group brought
your country its freedom.

Letters to my children #146

You will recognise a generous family by one trait: they make more food than for their family alone.

Letters to my children #147

I wish to be clear; I do not want to be kept alive on a machine. Pull the plug.

Letters to my children #148

Never beg. Ask without apology.

Letters to my children #149

The day you stop learning is the day you've died.

Letters to my children #150

Never argue when you're tired; you
will be playing with fire.

Letters to my children #151

If you respond angrily to someone because of who they are rather than what they did, you have a serious problem.

Letters to my children #152

Learn to lean on stronger shoulders; do not bear your pain alone.

Letters to my children #153

No matter how much doubt you have, give every person ONE chance to prove themselves.

Letters to my children #154

If you decide beforehand not to forget,

you have not really forgiven.

Letters to my children #155

Never confuse a religious experience
with a spiritual experience; one of them
is truly fulfilling.

Letters to my children #156

Do not respond to every sleight and provocation; remain focused on what is important.

Letters to my children #157

Do not confuse eloquence with
intelligence.

Letters to my children #158

When you do public speaking, watch the body language of your audience; it is the best sign of when to shut up.

Letters to my children #159

I need to warn you that the worst bigots
I have encountered in my life were
among the people who go to church.

Letters to my children #160

There will be days when everything seems to go wrong at the same time; it is then that your real character is being tested.

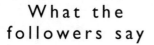

What the followers say

Feedback from followers and friends

I have included a small sample of the feedback, which I have received on Facebook and Twitter, to the letters to give the non-social media-literate readers a sense of the interaction that the letters have encouraged. I've kept the comments in the language in which they were submitted – mostly English or Afrikaans, but also the 'text-speak' that has become commonplace on social networks – and have only changed the language when it was difficult to follow. The feedback was not submitted anonymously, but I have not published the names of respondents here for reasons of privacy.

Waar de drommel kom prof aan al die wyshede?

My dad always used to say … 'as julle ernstige dinge uit die pad moet kry – maak seker dat albei van julle eers in die bed lê' :-)

So true … Pa Maasdorp always said, 'Ons is elke dag in 'n skool, en ons moet bereid wees om elke dag te leer.'

Prof that is so true – my late Dad used to say in Greek, 'I am not crying that I am dying but while I am alive I will learn.' He has made a great impact on my life, that is why I fight everyday with my sons – let it be a lifelong learning process …

Really? Sounds a bit pushy and arrogant.

No prof i disagree with u … jst dat u hate ANC …

Thought-provoking stuff, my former dean at Tuks.

Cross-cultural anything is enlightened?

Words of wisdom Prof!

I beg 2differ. God knws why he put you on earth, its who you destined 2b. In the end, u become hu u wer meant 2b.

You are given grace but not destiny?

Prof from the bottom of my heart I thank you for your shining example as a human and wisdom I so badly needed every time I felt down. A great honour to be on your friendlist!

Oh, I SO love this!

Now really, I can't get enough of Prof J's 'Letters to my children'. Where can I get a book of all the letters? Is there a book?